THE WILLIE LYNCH LETTER AND THE MAKING OF A SLAVE

THE WILLIE LYNCH LETTER

African Tree Press
The Willie Lynch Letter and the Making of a Slave

African Tree Press
PO Box 2085
Long Island City, NY 11102

ISBN: 1-59232-306-5

PRINTED IN THE UNITED STATES OF AMERICA

The first Africans in America arrived through Jamestown, Virginia in 1619, as indentured labor or servants.

From about 1619 to 1640, the laws throughout Europe and the Americas removed all human individuality from abducted Africans and named them property. The U.S. Supreme Court and chief justices like Roger B. Taney ensured that the law did not protect slaves, but imbued their white oppressors who physically, mentally and psychologically abused them with full supremacy.

"No Negro whether slave or free, could ever be considered a citizen of the United States..." the "honorable" judge wrote.

In 1640, Maryland became the first colony to institutionalize slavery in America and in 1641, Massachusetts, in its written legislation, titled: *Body of Liberties*, stated that "bondage was legal servitude", at that moment changing the status of the African hostages, to automatic chattel slaves, that could be bought and sold at the discretion of their white owners.

The Willie Lynch Letter

Gentlemen, I greet you here on the bank of the James River in the year of our Lord One Thousand Seven Hundred and Twelve. First, I shall thank you, the gentlemen of the Colony of Virginia, for bringing me here. I am here to help you solve some of your problems with slaves. Your invitation reached me on my modest plantation in the West Indies where I have experimented with some of the newest and still the oldest methods for control of slaves. Ancient Rome would envy us if my program is implemented.

As our boat sailed south on the James River, named for our illustrious King, whose version of the Bible we cherish, I saw enough to know that your problem is not unique. While Rome used cords of wood as crosses for standing human bodies along its old highway in great numbers you here are using the tree and the rope on occasion.

I caught the whiff of a dead slave hanging from a tree a couple of miles back. You are not only losing valuable stock by hangings, you are having uprisings, slaves are running away, your crops are sometimes left in the fields too long for maximum profit, you suffer occasional fires, your animals are killed. Gentlemen, you know what your problems are. I do not need to elaborate. I am not here to enumerate your problems, I am here to introduce you to a method of solving them.

In my bag here, <u>I have a fool proof method for controlling your Black slaves,</u> I guarantee every one of you that if installed correctly, <u>it will control the slaves for at least 300 hundred years.</u> My method is simple. Any member of your family or your overseer can use it.

I have outlined a number of differences among the slaves and I take these differences and make them bigger. I use fear, distrust, and envy for control purposes. These methods have worked on my modest plantation in the West Indies and it will work throughout the South.

7

Take this simple little list of differences, and think about them.

On top of my list is "Age" but it is there only because it starts with an "A": the second is "Color" or shade, there is intelligence, size, sex, status on plantation, attitude of owners, whether the slaves live in the valley, on a hill, East, West, North, South, have fine hair coarse hair, or is tall or short. Now that you have a list of differences, <u>I shall give you an outline of action-but before that I shall assure</u> you that distrust is stronger than trust, and envy is stronger than adulteration, respect or admiration.

The Black slave after receiving this indoctrination shall carry on and will become self re-fueling and self generating for hundreds of years, maybe thousands.

Don't forget you must pitch the old Black male vs. the young Black male, and the young Black male against the old Black male. You must use the dark skin slaves vs. the light skin slaves and the light skin slaves vs. the dark skin slaves. You must also have your white servants and overseers distrust all Blacks, but <u>it is necessary that your slaves trust and depend on us. They must love, respect and trust only us.</u>

Gentlemen, these kits are your keys to control. Use them. Have your wives and children use them, never miss an opportunity. If used intensely for one year, the slaves themselves will remain perpetually distrustful. Thank you gentlemen.

LET'S MAKE A SLAVE

The Origin and Development of a Social Being Called "The Negro"

Let us make a slave. What do we need? First of all we need a black nigger man, a pregnant nigger woman and her baby nigger boy. Second, we will use the same basic principle that we use in breaking a horse, combined with some more sustaining factors. We reduce them from their natural state in nature; whereas nature provides them with the natural capacity to take care of their needs and the needs of their offspring, we break that natural string of independence from them and thereby create a dependency state so that we maybe able to get from them useful production for our business and pleasure.

CARDINAL PRINCIPLES FOR MAKING A NEGRO

For fear that our future generations may not understand the principles of breaking both horses and men, we lay down the art. For, if we are to sustain our basic economy we must break both of the beasts together, the nigger and the horse. We understand that short range planning in economics results in periodic economic chaos, so that, to avoid turmoil in the economy, it requires us to have breadth and depth in long range comprehensive planning, articulating both skill and sharp perception. We lay down the following principles for long range comprehensive economic planning:

1. Both horse and niggers are no good to the economy in the wild or natural state.
2. Both must be broken and tied together for orderly production.
3. For orderly futures, special and particular attention must be paid to the female and the youngest offspring.
4. Both must be crossbred to produce a variety and division of labor.
5. Both must be taught to respond to a peculiar new language.

6. Psychological and physical instruction of containment must be created for both.

We hold the above six cardinals as truths to be self-evident, based upon the following discourse concerning the economics of breaking and tying the horse and nigger together...all inclusive of the six principles laid down above.

NOTE: Neither principles alone will suffice for good economics. All principles must be employed for the orderly good of the nation. Accordingly, both a wild horse and a wild or natural nigger is dangerous even if captured, for they will have the tendency to seek their customary freedom, and, in doing so, might kill you in your sleep. You cannot rest. They sleep while you are awake and are awake while you are asleep. They are dangerous near the family house and it requires too much labor to watch them away from the house. Above all you cannot get them to work in this natural state. Hence, both the horse and the nigger must be broken, that is break them from one form of mental life to another,

"KEEP THE BODY AND TAKE THE MIND"

In other words, break the will to resist. Now the breaking process is the same for the

13

horse and the nigger, only slightly varying in degrees. But as we said before, You must keep your eye focused on the female and the offspring of the horse and the nigger. A brief discourse in offspring development will shed light on the key to sound economic principles. Pay little attention to the generation of original breaking but concentrate on future generations. Therefore, if you break the female, she will break the offspring in its early years of development and, when the offspring is old enough to work, she will deliver it up to you. For her normal female protective tendencies will have been lost in the original breaking process. For example, take the case of the wild stud horse, a female horse and an already infant horse and compare the breaking process with two captured nigger males in their natural state, a pregnant nigger woman with her infant offspring. Take the stud horse, break him for limited containment. Completely break the female horse until she becomes very gentle whereas you or anybody can ride her in comfort. Breed the mare and the stud until you have the desired offspring. Then you can turn the stud to freedom until you need him again. Train the female horse whereby she will eat out of your hand, and she will train the infant horse to eat out of your hand also.

When it comes to breaking the uncivilized nigger, use the same process, but vary the degree and step up the pressure so as to do a complete reversal of the mind. Take the meanest and most restless nigger, strip him of his clothes in front of the remaining male niggers, the female, and the nigger infant, tar and feather him, tie each leg to a different horse faced in opposite directions, set him afire and beat both horses to pull him apart in front of the remaining niggers.

The next step is to take a bullwhip and beat the remaining nigger male to the point of death in front of the female and the infant. Don't kill him. But put the fear of God in him, for he can be useful for future breeding.

THE BREAKING PROCESS OF THE AFRICAN WOMAN

Take the female and run a series of tests on her to see if she will submit to your desires willingly. Test her in every way, because she is the most important factor for good economics. If she shows any signs of resistance in submitting completely to your will, do not hesitate to use the bull whip on her to extract that last bit of bitch out of her. Take care not to kill her, for in doing so, you spoil good economics. When in complete submission, she will train her offspring in the early years to submit to labor when they become of age.

Understanding is the best thing. Therefore, we shall go deeper into this area of the subject matter concerning what we have produced here in this breaking of the female nigger. We have reversed the relationships. In her natural uncivilized state she would have a strong dependency on the uncivilized nigger male, and she would have a limited protective dependency toward her independent male offspring and would raise female offspring to be dependent like her. Nature had provided for this type of balance. We reversed nature by burning and pulling one civilized nigger apart and bull whipping the other to the point of death—all in her presence. By her being left alone, unprotected, with the male image destroyed, the ordeal caused her to move from her psychological dependent state to a frozen independent State. In this frozen psychological state of independence she will raise her male and female offspring in reversed roles. For fear of the young male's life she will psychologically train him to be mentally weak and dependent but physically strong.

Because she has become psychologically independent, she will train her female offspring to be psychological independent as well. What have you got? You've got the nigger woman out front and the nigger man behind and scared. This is a perfect situation for sound sleep and economics.

Before the breaking process, we had to be alert and on guard at all times. Now we can sleep soundly, for out of frozen fear, his woman stands guard for us. He cannot get past her early infant slave molding process. He is a good tool, now ready to be tied to the horse at a tender age.

By the time a nigger boy reaches the age of sixteen, he is soundly broken in and ready for a long life of sound and efficient work and the reproduction of a unit of good labor force.

Continually, through the breaking of uncivilized savage niggers, by throwing the nigger female savage into a frozen psychological state of independency, by killing the protective male image, and by creating a submissive dependent mind of the nigger male slave, we have created an orbiting cycle that turns on its own axis forever, unless a phenomenon occurs and re-shifts the positions of the male and female savages. We show what we mean by example. Take the case of the two economic slave units and examine them closely.

THE NEGRO MARRIAGE UNIT

We breed two nigger males with two nigger females. Then we take the nigger males away from them and keep them moving and working. Say the nigger female bears a nigger female and the other bears a nigger male. Both nigger females, being without influence of the nigger male image, frozen with an independent psychology, will raise their offspring into reverse positions. The one with the female offspring will teach her to be like herself, independent and negotiable (we negotiate with her, through her, by her, and negotiate her at will) The one with the nigger male offspring, she being frozen with a subconscious fear for his life, will raise him to be mentally dependent and weak, but physically strong...in other words, body over mind. Now, in a few years when these two offspring become fertile for early reproduction, we will mate and breed them and continue the cycle. That is good, sound, and long range comprehensive planning.

WARNING: POSSIBLE INTERLOPING NEGATIVES

Earlier, we talked about the non-economic good of the horse and the nigger in their wild or natural state; we talked out the principle of breaking and tying them together for orderly production, furthermore, we talked about paying particular attention to the female savage and her offspring for orderly future planning; then more recently we stated that, by reversing the positions of the male and the female savages we had created an orbiting cycle that turns on its own axis forever, unless phenomenon occurred, and re shifted the positions of the male and female savages.

Our experts warned us about the possibility of this phenomenon occurring, for they say that the mind has a strong drive to correct and re-correct itself over a period of time if it can touch some substantial original historical base; and they advised us that the best way to deal with this phenomenon is to shave off the brute's mental history and create a multiplicity of phenomenon or illusions so that each illusion will twirl in its own orbit, something akin to floating balls in a vacuum.

This creation of a multiplicity of phenomenon or illusions entails the principles of crossbreeding the nigger and the horse as we stated above, the purpose of which is to create a diversified division of labor. The results of which is the severance of the points of original beginning's for each spherical illusion. Since we feel that the subject matter may get more complicated as we proceed in laying down our economic plan concerning the purpose, reason, and effect of cross-breeding horses and niggers, we shall lay down the following definitional terms for future generations.

I. Orbiting cycle means a thing turning in a given pattern.

2. Axis means upon which or around which a body turns.

3. Phenomenon means something beyond ordinary conception and inspires awe and wonder.

4. Multiplicity means a great number.

5. Sphere means a globe.

6. Cross-breeding a horse means taking a horse and breeding it with an ass and you get a dumb backward ass, longheaded mule that is not reproductive nor productive by itself.

7. Cross-breeding niggers means taking so many drops of good white blood and putting them into as many nigger women as possible, varying the drops by the

various tones that you want, and then letting them breed with each other until the circle of colors appear as you desire.

What this means is this: Put the niggers and the horse in the breeding pot, mix some asses and some good white blood and what do you get? You got a multiplicity of colors of ass backwards, unusual niggers, running, tied to backwards ass longheaded mules, the one productive of itself, the other sterile. (The one constant, the other dying. We keep the nigger constant for we may replace the mule for another tool) both mule and nigger tied to each other, neither knowing where the other came from and neither productive for itself, nor without each other.

CONTROLLED LANGUAGE

Cross-breeding completed, for further severance from their original beginning, we must completely annihilate the mother tongue of both the nigger and the new mule and institute a new language that involves the new life's work of both. You know, language is a peculiar institution. It leads to the heart of a people. The more a foreigner knows about the language of another country the more he is able to move through all levels of that society.

Therefore, if the foreigner is an enemy of the country, to the extent that he knows the body of the language, to that extent is the country vulnerable to attack or invasion of a foreign culture. For example, you take a slave, if you teach him all about your language, he will know all your secrets, and he is then no more a slave, for you can't fool him any longer and having a fool is one of the basic ingredients of and incidents to the making of the slavery system.

For example if you told a slave that he must perform in getting out "our crops" and he knows the language well, he would know that "our crops" didn't mean "our" crops, and the slavery system would break down, for he would relate on the basis of what "our crops " Really meant. So you have to be careful in setting up new language for the slave would soon be in your house, talking to you as "man to man" and that is death to our economic system. In addition, the definition of words or terms are only a minute part of the process. Values are created and transported by communication through the body of the language. A total society has many interconnected value system. All these values in the society have bridges of language to connect them for orderly working in the society. But for these language bridges, these many value systems would sharply clash and cause internal-strife or civil war, the degree of the conflict being determined by the magnitude of the issues or relative opposing strength in whatever for. For example, if you put a slave in a hog pen and train him to live there and incorporate in him to value it as a way of life completely, the biggest problem you would have out of him is that he would worry you about provisions to keep the hog pen clean, or partially clean, or he might not worry you at all.

On the other hand, if you put this same slave in the same hog pen and make a slip and incorporate them for something in his language whereby he comes to value a house more than he does his hog pen, you got a problem.

"He will soon be in your house!!!"

Made in the USA
San Bernardino, CA
05 September 2019